PRAISE FOR *WAKE UP!*

David Krieger has spent a lifetime working for peace. As long as we can hear his voice, now in the clarion call of his poetry, there will remain hope for man on Earth.

~**Gerry Spence**, author of *From Freedom to Slavery*

Wake Up! is accessible and moving writing, setting itself against the dominant murderous culture of our time. Every poem hits home.

~**Lawrence Ferlinghetti**, poet, author of *A Coney Island of the Mind*

If you thought that David Krieger had passion only for peace and nuclear disarmament, then you were wrong. Another passion of his is writing poetry and he does this equally well. *Wake Up!* Challenges its readers to awaken, engage the world, and become a force for global peace and justice. There is haunting beauty and truth in this poetry.

~**Archbishop Desmond Tutu,** Nobel Peace Laureate

Wake Up! is a love song to hope and the human spirit, written by a deep soul whose cosmic perspective sheds light on our most serious human problems. David Krieger embodies the highest duty of the poet by revealing beauty in unexpected places and challenging the attitudes that sustain war and injustice. These poems summon what is best in humanity and weave a vision that can inspire, transform, and awaken us.

~**Paul K. Chappell,** author of *The Art of Waging Peace*

Poetic reflections on what most afflicts the planet as well as on the acts of spirit and will that redeem humanity. David Krieger heeds healing ancient wisdom while celebrating brave peace warriors, lamenting solemn war makers.

~**Richard Falk,** Professor Emeritus of International Law and Practice, Princeton University

David Krieger's latest collection of poems, *Wake Up!*, reads like a series of eloquent telegrams sent directly to the heart of a culture, ours, that has been conditioned to avoid at all costs the distasteful burden of responsibility. Children are dying at our hands. Krieger more than knows that—he feels it. But rather than wring his hands, he deals out startling lines of finely hewn poetry designed to jolt us out of our complacency. David Krieger's work continues to seek that razor-edged eloquence needed to pierce the husk around America's collective psyche. His clarity of vision, his unremitting integrity shines through these pages.

~**Doug Rawlings**, poet and Vietnam War veteran

With *Wake Up!*, David Krieger, "poet laureate of the Nuclear Age," continues to celebrate life and calls upon the conscience of humanity to end killing, war and the threat of nuclear extinction. In his voice of democratic compassion inspired by nature we hear a powerful 21st century echo of Walt Whitman. Truly an inspiring, creative work.

~**Glenn Paige,** founder of the Center for Global Non-Killing

Wake Up! is a moving and inspiring new book of poetry by David Krieger. It reveals the heart of a man of compassion and peace.

~**Mairead Maguire,** Nobel Peace Laureate

David Krieger, perhaps the most prolific poet on the subject of peace, minces no words in this powerful latest collection. He confronts those who choose war and its atrocities over preferred peace making methods, and invites the complacent to *Wake Up!* "while there is still time, while we still can." If poetry could save us, his poems certainly would.

~**Perie Longo,** Santa Barbara Poet Laureate Emerita

Thanks to David Krieger for lovingly waking us up as a suicidal cult becomes viral without our advice or consent. Drones, missiles and biocidal nuclear ovens are now over funded. Yes, we can stop them before they kill again. We can accept the demise of the butterflies and the children, or choose to rise from our sleep.

~**Blase Bonpane,** co-founder and
Director of Office of the Americas

What a collection! Krieger's poetry stands against war, and his powerful satire and symbolism for peace create hope.

~**Stuart Rees**, founder, Sydney
Peace Foundation

POETRY BOOKS BY DAVID KRIEGER

Wake Up!

God's Tears:
Reflections on the Atomic Bombs
Dropped on Hiroshima and Nagasaki

The Doves Flew High

Today Is Not a Good Day for War

Edited Volumes

Summer Grasses:
An Anthology of War Poetry

Never Enough Flowers:
The Poetry of Peace II
(with Perie Longo)

The Poetry of Peace

WAKE UP!

DAVID KRIEGER

A Nuclear Age Peace Foundation Book
1187 Coast Village Road, Suite 1, PMB 121
Santa Barbara, California 93108

ISBN: 150098874X
ISBN-13: 9781500988746

First Edition

To those who say No to war
and Yes to peace

To Veterans for Peace

The soldiers threw their medals back.
They fell on the ground clickety-clack.

"Since Auschwitz we know what man is capable of. And since Hiroshima we know what is at stake."

~Victor Frankl

"For the first time in history, the physical survival of the human race depends on a radical change of the human heart."

~Erich Fromm

CONTENTS

WAR

REMEMBERING BUSH II

IMPERFECTION

To Write Poetry

"To write poetry after Auschwitz is barbaric."
~Theodor Adorno

Adorno had it wrong.

After Auschwitz, poetry is needed more than ever, but no longer has the luxury of being trivial. And it is not only after Auschwitz, but also after Hiroshima and Nagasaki, and the wars, genocides and threats of universal death following World War II.

Those who write poetry after Auschwitz must confront the ugliness of our human brutality. They must express the heart's longing for peace and reveal its grief at our loss of decency. They must uncover the truth of who we are behind our masks and who we could become.

After Auschwitz, it is not poetry or art that is barbaric. It is genocide and war and violence of every kind that are barbaric. It is each of us, each a part of the whole, that is barbaric.

To write poetry after Auschwitz is to hold up a mirror to our shame and sorrow, and to provide a path for our promise. It is to probe a way forward, to forgive without forgetting and to find new ways of keeping hope alive, even in the face of the tragic reality of our shared history. Poetry can uncover truths that can reconnect us with ourselves and with our lost humanity.

A country that does not appreciate poetry is a country without a way of finding its soul. A world that does not appreciate poetry is a world enmeshed in chaos and violence, a world without a way of finding a decent future.

David Krieger

TRUTH IS BEAUTY

Six Views of the Moon

Slice of moon –
so much missing
from our view

Cloudless sky –
no place for the moon
to hide

Autumn night –
the moon
wears a yellow veil

Its simple beauty –
an orange moon
on a dark night

Still afloat
in the morning sky –
last night's moon

Most amazing –
I can still be amazed
by a lonely moon

Boundaries

Above us, a full expanse of night sky
unfurled in splendor, the white moon
ringed by a halo of ice, stars touching
the tips of the sea, waves murmuring
against the shore, boundaries unbound,
overcome by destiny and imagination.

And looking back from the vastness
of space, there is a lonely planet,
a blue-green water planet teeming with life,
without boundaries, without precedent,
far more rare and precious than the tears
of all its emperors.

The Mystery of Fog

On this quiet morning, a heavy fog
has settled over the sea. The islands
off the coast have disappeared.

We have walked this trail so many times
we know the shape of what is behind the fog.

Our minds hold a place for what is missing,
no matter how thick or dark the fog,

Behind the veil, I am certain of this:
there never was, nor will be, a country, a flag,
worth a single human life.

Sorrow

We can move a glacier,
but we cannot force the snow to fall.
Where we once walked across the frozen straights
the thin ice cracks and melts.

Our sorrow spreads across borders.
It has become our stability.
We pray the Earth can withstand our assault,
but who is listening?

We have insulted the gods, trespassed
On the fortress of their solitude.
At the center of the thirsty sky, the sun stands still.

Ultima Thule

In that last and farthest place
no bold beauty coldly shown
abides in sleek metallic forms
of death full-blown, aching
to be hurled across the star-filled
skies. What is in that far space,
but purest heart where truth resides
that conquers base and needless lies.
In that land, so distant and extreme,
dwells a sweet and simple decency,
rare on our too familiar Earth,
a decency as found in subtle dreams
of hope and love's rebirth.

Hamburg

Delicate clouds sweep by –
the fresh snow white
on sloped roofs

Snow all around –
the violinist pierces
the cold gray morning

Church of Saint Nikolai –
destroyed in war, silent
sentinel of peace

In the black night
snowflakes flutter down
upon our dreams

The Clarity of Winter

Today the blue ocean is alive
and the islands offshore rise from the sea
like an armada sailing home, another cause
for celebrating some distant and minor victory.
Our generation has lived through so many
of these sailings, so many bloody victories
at sea and on the land that we have lost
our perspective, become unsure of the horizon,
unsteady as an ocean of ignorance and lies rises
and falls around us. The view has made us dizzy,
caused us to lower our eyes and look away
from the crimes of empire. In this dullness
of spirit we carry the burdens of the past ever
so lightly. Unlike those who fought with stones
and spears and arrows, we are long-distance killers
fighting with drones and missiles. The seas, the air,
the land are full of our fancy technologies of death.
In the clarity of winter, one need only look inward
to know we are failing ourselves and the future,
one need only sense the sun pausing in its arc across
the pale blue sky.

Taught by Time

Time carries no pretense of progress
nor perfection.

It cares not where it has been
but plods ahead with measured strides.

Each moment, filled with rich potential,
is the same as each before.

Time has no stops nor starts nor curves
nor rapids like a rushing torrent.

It is a moving slate
from which no safe escape is possible.

We may revel in our freedom,
yet time holds us all prisoners.

Its steady drip falls and falls again
upon our stately, or not so stately, souls.

It is a patient teacher whose voice
by force must be our own.

Inherited Hope

"We've inherited hope – the gift of forgetting."
~Wislawa Symborska

If only we could forget it all –
every slaughter, war and execution.
We could wipe our slates clean
and be proud of who we are.

But then we would repeat our acts
of unforgivable violence over and over.
And, although we had forgotten the past,
we would daily despair our present.

The gift of forgetting –
such a grand contribution to hope.
Most of history already disappeared
beneath the censor's black pen.

Could we not, just once, earn our hope
by the struggle for peace?
Could we not, for once, try walking
that narrow, winding dangerous path?

A Sage Walks Slowly

We hang from well-worn threads
of life, embedded in a fragile web.

We are the weavers and the woven.
In tenacity of being, we've been chosen.

We daily choose among the voices
offering strange Confucian choices.

At times, a man must take a stand,
must take the future in his hands.

The winds are fierce and bitter cold
and we grow sad and we grow old.

Wandering through fresh fields of war
we plant our flags, we lose our core.

A sage walks slowly, straight and proud,
faces life with head unbowed.

A Few Simple Truths

Life is the universe's most precious creation.

There is only one place we know of where life exists.

Children, all children, deserve a full and fair chance.

The bomb threatens all life.

War is legitimized murder with collateral damage.

Construction requires more than a hammer.

The rising of the oceans cannot be contained by money.

Love is the only currency that truly matters.

One true human brings beauty to the Earth.

Somehow

"Somehow this madness must cease."
~Martin Luther King, Jr.

Somehow, like a small stunned bird
cupped in our hands with its heart racing,
is a word of hope or desperation,

carrying a moral burden, a Sisyphean burden,
to do whatever is possible, before
it is too late.

Might we not somehow awaken,
open our eyes, stand up in the face of madness
and, even on trembling legs

with a fluttering heart, comfort
the small bird until it can spread its wings
and fly away?

It is a delicate task to set aside
the blanket of complacency, to somehow,
as he did, clutch courage to our breast.

The Last Words of Dr. Seuss

He said it simply.
No rhyme, much reason.

Perhaps his wires got crossed
with Kurt Vonnegut.
It wasn't a warning, or was it?

He took a deep gasping breath
before moving on and said:

"We can do better than this."

Polishing Buddha

Clouds carry the rain.
Rain cleanses the earth.
Earth, sun and rain nourish
plants that nourish us.
We are a part of the whole, and
the whole is a part of us, here
on this blue-green island of life.
When we are compassionate
to the weak and frail, to even the ants,
as Schweitzer was, we are polishing
our peaceful Buddha, who, with eyes
cast down, feels the world's pain,
yet remains calm, hopeful,
knowing we can still save, if not all,
at least some part of the beauty, some part
of the truth.

WAR

Little Changes

Our brave young soldiers
shot babies at My Lai –
few remember.

Lieutenant Calley –
sentenced to house arrest
until pardoned by Nixon.

Then it was *gooks.*
Now it is *hajjis* –
little changes.

Abu Ghraib –
the buck stops nowhere.
It still hasn't stopped.

From My Lai
to Abu Ghraib –
the terrible silence.

Soldiers Fall

War spreads
its sad red wings.

Soldiers fall
like white flowers
on a winter field.

They sink
in burning snow.

Mother to Daughter, Buchenwald 1944

Child, the world will be the world again.

Hold tight to this thought, embrace it.
The bitter grayness of senseless death
will not last forever.

Water the tree of hope with your tears.
Child, the fruit of this tree grows
even in darkness.

One day this fruit will be ready to harvest.
On that day, in the magic of life, this place
will be as distant as the stars.

Bombing Gaza: A Pilot Speaks

The stain of death spreads below,
but from my cockpit I see none of it.
I only drop bombs as I have been trained
and then, far above the haze and blood,
I speed toward home.

I am deaf to the screams of pain.
Nor can I smell the stench of slaughter.
I try not to think of children shivering
with fear or of those blown to pieces.

They tell me I am brave, but
how brave can it be to drop bombs
on a crowded city? I am a cog,
only that, a cog in a fancy machine
of death.

Norman Morrison

November 2, 1965

Sitting calmly before the Pentagon, like a Buddhist monk,
he doused himself in kerosene, lit a match and went up in flame.

I imagine McNamara, stiff and unflinching, as he watched
from above.

To his wife, Morrison wrote, "Know that I love thee,
but I must go to help the children of the priest's village."

When it happened, the wife of the YMCA director said,
"I can understand a heathen doing that, but not a Christian."

Few Americans remember his name, but in Vietnam
children still sing songs about his courage.

A General Plans for Battle

Here is the battlefield, here are the pawns
(I mean soldiers).
Our boys have that intangible desire to win.
I doubt that they would run away.
They know how to puff themselves up
to look fierce. Their screams are the cries
of wild men, louder than machineguns or bombs.
Their bayonets are razor sharp and deadly.
Our boys will advance on order, ready to kill
and give their young lives.
Soon our boys will be put to a terrible test.
Surely, God will protect us. Surely, my brilliance
will carry the day.

Rules of Engagement

"Golden like a shower." ~U.S. Marine

Three Afghan men lay dead on their backs in the dirt.
Above them, four U.S. Marines in battle gear celebrate
by urinating on them. These young Marines
with their golden showers are holding up a mirror
to America. It reminds us: *this is who we are.*

When we teach our children to kill we turn them
into something we don't understand: ourselves.
Their lack of humanity is not different from ours.
We have not taught these young men to value life,
but they are teaching us how little we do.

Why should they hold back when we have
taught them and sent them to kill other men –
men whose names they will never know?
If we are shocked by their disrespect for the dead,
we should consider our own for the living.

The Torturers

The torturers will gather in Hades.

There will be no pleasantries.

They will be stripped of all honors.

They will be awakened
to the baseness of their crimes.

They will be purged of all justifications.

Their smiles will be banished.

They will see their true faces.

They will be surrounded by the screams
of their victims.

They will understand who they are.

Of Hawks and Drones

A red-tailed hawk soars and circles
above the tall trees and silent fields
looking down for movement, for prey.
Gray clouds press against nearby mountains.
From another direction the sun lights up
the fields and mountainside.

Somewhere in an innocuous, but not innocent,
place in the United States of America,
a young military officer stares intently
at a computer screen. He operates
the remote control of a predator drone flying
softly above houses in Pakistan, but it could be
anywhere.

The predator drone is armed with precision missiles
that the young officer releases above the target
he has been given. People die.

They are not always the right people. Sometimes
they are children. Sometimes the information
is wrong, the coordinates are mistaken.

The red-tailed hawk glides on currents of thin air,
then dives toward Earth, talons at the ready.

Missile Test

Black.
The night is black.
No moon, no stars.

We protest
a missile launch, testing
a land-based intercontinental ballistic missile

capable of carrying
a nuclear-armed warhead to the far corners
of our sad globe.

Shortly after midnight
we walk onto the roadway of the military base
in protest.

The young airmen are polite
as they handcuff us, search us and put us
carefully into vans.

When the missile is later launched
we don't see its fiery tail – the 15 of us
under arrest that night.

We cannot see it streak away
under the cover of darkness
in the black of night, in the ocean fog.

A half-hour after launch
the missile thuds into the surprised ocean
in the Marshall Islands.

Black.
The night is black.
No moon, no stars.

Bulldozers

In Desert Storm, an American war,
the U.S. military put bulldozer blades on its tanks
and buried Iraqi soldiers alive in desert sands.
This deserves more than a footnote in the annals
of human cruelty.

Rachel Corrie, a young American, stood
before an Israeli bulldozer that threatened the home
of a Palestinian family. She refused to give way.
This deserves more than a footnote in the annals
of human courage.

Archeology of War

The years of war numb us, grind us
down as they pile up one upon the other
forming a burial mound not only
for the fallen soldiers and innocents
who were killed, but for the parts of us,
once decent and bright with hope,
now deflated by the steady fall of death
and sting of empty promises.

Think and Think Again

In the revolution, men fought
for cause and country, not for a lie.

In the Great War, they say
the best young men followed the flag,
fought in the trenches and died
on the barbed-wire fields of battle.
A generation was more than lost.
It was destroyed.

In our generation
the bravest young men went to prison
and served their time. They refused
to salute, carry a rifle, and kill peasants
in jungles on the far side of the world.

The worst of our generation also refused
to fight. They gathered deferments
until they could walk away in safety.
Strange that these are the ones,
the Cheneys, who found old ways
to bring new generations to war.

Young men, learn history and think
and think again. Too many have died,
not for cause and country, but for a lie.

Similarities 1914 and 2014

The countries of Europe, it is said,
stumbled into World War I, a war
no one wanted and yet, and yet…it happened.
After Archduke Franz Ferdinand's assassination,
it became the Great War, taking the lives
of a generation of young men too eager to fight
in the battlefield trenches.

What can we say about the confrontation
of great powers, going on at this very moment,
in Ukraine? Could the leaders of these countries
be stumbling again, this time on a powder
keg of nuclear alliance, misunderstandings,
irrationality, false promises, political realities
and unrealities, indignation and, above all,
bravado, as always, bravado for God and country?

Oh, War

Oh, war, let us count the ways we'll use you.
To profit, to add excitement to the dullness of our lives,
to unite our country, to make our young men dashing,
to profit, to give new meaning to our lives, to prove
ourselves on fields of battle, to stimulate our poets,
to rally round our flag, to bring forth the eloquence
of our leaders, to defeat the barbarians, to add medals
to our uniforms, to profit, to put us to the test of battle,
to defend what we love most, to conquer, to save
our leaders from the compromise of peace, to expand
our territory, to use our weapons and create new ones,
to profit, to heighten love by loss, to sacrifice, to add
glory to our history, to love more deeply, to protect
our oil supply, to immortalize ourselves, to profit.

When the Killing Stops

Our army is powerful.
It maims and it kills.
But where has our humanity gone?

When the killing stops
we declare victory
without weighing the bitterness.

We will not regain our humanity
by pinning medals on those
who pulled the triggers.

We will not find our lost souls
while we prepare
for our next onslaught.

Our army is powerful.
It shoots and it bombs.
But where has our humanity gone?

Children of War

In war, children die,
float away on clouds of grief.
By far, the greatest lie of all
is the well-worn but absurd belief
that war is noble, not a crime.

In war, children writhe in pain,
while their parents wail.
Before we spread war's red stain,
should we not consider how we fail
the young, again and yet again?

The Chorus of Children Sings

Your bombs make such loud noise.
They hurt our hearts. They tear us apart.
Your bombs are powerful, but so are our hearts.

We only want to live as children.
We are sick of the bombs you drop on us.
Will you stop? Will you ever stop?

REMEMBERING BUSH II

Leader of the Free World

I am a wily white-skinned man
with a wicked grin and ready hand.
I am the Man.

I tell the generals who to bomb
and they do it with aplomb.
I keep the world orderly.

When people come to call on me
they bring along their money.
I am the Man.

I never studied hard in school.
Parties were the only rule
that mattered much to me.

I decide who lives, who dies
so that corporate profits rise.
I am the Man.

Since freedom isn't really free
I've had to sacrifice democracy
and rescind your liberty.

I am special, unlike you.
God always tells me what to do.
I am the Man.

Searching for a Soul

This country once had a soul, perhaps it can
again.

It would have to look very hard, through the eyes
of its people.

The people would need to get down on their hands
and knees to search.

But what if they found only lapel pins that looked
like flags?

What if they found only bombs bursting in air?

Zero Tolerance

"We will not tolerate any deception,
denial or deceit, period."
~George W. Bush, November 13, 2002

Tell us, then, where you first learned of evil
and how many men you have killed.

Tell us the secrets you've inherited
and hidden behind your smirk.

Tell us about the Axis of Arrogance,
about Cheney and Rumsfeld and Rice.

Tell us where the vice-president is hidden
and what he is hiding from us.

Tell us why oil is so valuable
and life so cheap in your hands.

Tell us all of your empty dreams
and why you're so eager for war.

Not the Other Way Around

"This war came to us, not the other way around."
~Condoleezza Rice, May 15, 2005

This war came to us as we massed troops
on the Iraqi border, half way around the world,

as we imagined weapons of mass destruction
behind every palace wall,

came to us unexpectedly, only after a proper
manipulation of intelligence.

This war came to us as we invaded Iraq,
as we executed our "shock and awe"

bombing plan, came to us on Orwell's pen,
Cheney's lies, Rumsfeld's arrogance

and Bush's cowardice. This war came to us
through a thousand imagined dangers,

through dreams of victory and precious oil.
It was surely not the other way around.

Autumn

God whispered in George Bush's ear.
Then came shock and awe.
The war president strutted in triumph.

Now two and a half years have passed.
American troops have been dying steadily
like water dripping from an autumn leaf.

Two thousand American troops are dead.
Not many compared to the Iraqi dead,
or to the scattered leaves of autumn.
But it is two-thirds of those who died on 9/11.

These deaths are used to justify the next deaths,
and on and on, while anguished cries of grief
echo through this darkened land,
while rain-soaked autumn leaves keep falling.

Waiting for an Answer

"My son died for nothing...."
~Cindy Sheehan

She mourned her son's death in a war
with no meaning.
The president said her son died for a noble cause,
so she asked the president, "What is the noble cause?"
And she set up camp near the president's Crawford ranch
to await an answer.

While the president sped by in his caravan of black SUVs,
and went bicycle riding with Lance Armstrong, and took naps,
enjoying yet another wartime vacation, and while more
mothers' sons died in the war, she waited and wilted
in the hot Texas sun.

The president never stopped to talk to this mother waiting
for an answer. When the press asked the president about her,
he replied, "I've got a life to live...."

Zaid's Misfortune

Zaid had the misfortune
of being born in Iraq, a country
rich with oil.

Iraq had the misfortune
of being invaded by a country
greedy for oil.

The country greedy for oil
had the misfortune of being led
by a man too eager for war.

Zaid's misfortune multiplied
when his parents were shot down
in front of their medical clinic.

Being eleven and haunted
by the deaths of one's parents
is a great misfortune.

In Zaid's misfortune
a distant silence engulfs
the sounds of war.

Greeting Bush in Baghdad

"This is a farewell kiss, you dog."
~Muntader al-Zaifdi

You are a guest in my country, unwanted
surely, but still a guest.

You stand before us waiting for praise,
but how can we praise you?

You come after your planes have rained
death on our cities.

Your soldiers broke down our doors,
humiliated our men, disgraced our women.

We are not a frontier town and you are not
our marshal.

You are a torturer. We know you force water
down the throats of our prisoners.

We have seen the pictures of our naked prisoners
threatened by your snarling dogs.

You are a maker of widows and orphans,
a most unwelcome guest.

I have only this for you, my left shoe that I hurl
at your lost and smirking face,

and my right shoe that I throw at your face
of no remorse.

Staying the Course

The race has been run
and he lost.

Yet, he swaggers
around the track as though
it were a victory lap.

It is hard not to think:
How pathetic is power.

Falcon

Our space-age, nuclear-age,
information-age, age of hypocrisy
is filled with acronyms.

If it can extract money from taxpayers,
chances are it has an acronym
and will be honed for death.

Falcon stands for "Force Application and Launch
from CONUS," and is so hot it has an acronym
within an acronym, CONUS
standing for Continental United States.

This year Falcon gets $100 million to develop
a reusable Hypersonic Cruise Vehicle,
also known as an HCV.

Falcon will deliver a conventional,
precision-guided warhead anywhere, that's right
anywhere, up to 9,000 miles
from the Continental United States.

Just pick your target, and Falcon
will deliver its six ton payload
in less than two hours.

The magical Falcon will be launched into space,
fly to its target, pluck out the hearts
of its unsuspecting victims, and return
to the waiting arm of its handler,

a man like Cheney with a black eye patch.

Election Day

This is the People's Day, their chance
to choose a leader.

The excitement rustles in the leaves.

Even the sun is excited, even the snow.

An era is ending. History's fool is going home.

So is his crazy, criminal, mean-spirited number two.

Now the choice is simple: transformation or more
of the same.

The people in the long lines are waiting for their chance
to choose.

Yesterday we suffered, tomorrow may be the same.

But today there is anticipation, a choice for our dreams.

Today we can be better than we are.

GLOBAL HIROSHIMA

The Four Seasons of Hiroshima

Summer
A quiet morning
Suddenly the sun explodes

Autumn
The people wander
Through the ash

Winter
Without the sun
The cold penetrates

Spring
The grasses return
And the plum blossoms

Among the Ashes

Among the ashes
of Hiroshima
were crisply charred bodies.

In one of the charred bodies
a daughter recognized
the gold tooth of her mother.

As the girl reached out
to touch the burnt body
her mother crumbled to ashes.

Her mother, so vivid
in the girl's memory, sifted
through her hands, floated away.

A Grandmother's Story

The grandmother looked into the eyes
of her granddaughter, recalling the day
the bomb dropped on Hiroshima.

The sky was bluest blue, she said.
And when the sky exploded
the wind knocked me off my feet.

All around me there were screams
that still echo in my ears,
children calling for their mothers.

The wounded walked past us
with vacant stares, their skin hanging
like ribbons from their bodies.

Hiroshima became a city of death.
We lost all will to live until
new shoots of grass appeared.

With them, the darkness melted
into small green blades of hope.

In Hiroshima Peace Memorial Park

The heat of summer is oppressive.

Children pass by in groups, chattering.
They wear school outfits –
black pants or skirts and white shirts.

Some groups are wearing yellow caps.
They stop at Sadako's statue and,
in lilting voices, sing songs with words
I cannot understand.

When they finish their songs, they bow,
paying tribute to one of their own, Sadako,
forever young, a child of the bomb.

Though nearly seven decades have passed,
I feel guilty for what my country did here.

To whom can I apologize? To whom must
I apologize? It doesn't matter.
They have already forgiven, long ago.

A Tree for the Victims

As far away as London, there is a solid tree,
a stately tree, I would say, casting a broad shadow
on a cool green lawn.

A plaque at the base of the tree tells passers-by
that the tree was planted by the worshipful Mayor
of Camden, Councillor Mrs. Millie Miller,
on August 6, 1967.

It was twenty-two years after the new
U.S. bomb destroyed Hiroshima, killing ordinary people –
men, women and children – by blast, fire and radiation.
Some victims were incinerated, leaving only shadows.

How can a single tree, no matter how solid, bear
the weight of such memory?

Now, many years later, picnickers laugh and eat
their lunches in the shade of the tree.

Duck and Cover

circa 1950

Children,
this is the way you will be saved
from a nuclear attack. At the sound
of the bell you will scramble as fast
as you can under your desk.
Face downward toward the floor
in a kneeling position
with your head resting on your arms.
Keep your eyes squeezed
tightly shut, not opening them
or looking up until you hear me say
"All clear."

This is the way you will be saved
from shards of glass and other objects
traveling at speeds of hundreds of miles
per hour. And from the flash of white
light that could melt your eyeballs. And
from the explosion that could scramble
your brains and the rest of your organs.
And this is the way you will be saved
from the fire that may incinerate you,
leaving you shriveled, charred
and lifeless.

This is the way you will be saved
from the radiation that will cause your gums
to bleed, your hair to fall out, leukemia
to form in your blood, and lead
to either a slow and painful death,
or one more rapid and painful.
Pay close attention to these directions
so you will get it right the first time.

Seven Billion Reasons

Nuclear weapons
are frightful weapons.
They can destroy everything.

Each person on the planet,
each of seven billion, is a reason
to abolish these weapons.

Addie is one reason.
She is seven years old and wants to be
a cheerleader.

Nat is another reason.
He is ten years old and needs more time
to do his homework.

Alice is yet another reason.
She is only three years old.
She loves to make her friends laugh.

What is at risk is all of us
and all that humans have created
since we emerged as human.

Think about all you love and treasure.
Think about the uniqueness of life
in a vast universe.

Think about a lonely planet orbiting
a lonely star.

Another Hiroshima Day Has Passed

And there are still nuclear weapons in the world.

They are still on hair-trigger alert, weapons
with no concern for you or me or anyone.

They are weapons with steel hearts.
There is no bargaining with them.

They have nothing to say or perhaps
they speak in another language.
They do not speak our language.

They have only one battle plan
and that is utter destruction.

They have no respect for the laws of war
or any laws, even those of nature.

Another Hiroshima Day has passed
and the shadow of the bomb still darkens
the forests of our dreams.

Wake Up!

The alarm is sounding.
Can you hear it?

Can you hear the bells
of Nagasaki
ringing out for peace?

Can you feel the heartbeat
of Hiroshima
pulsing out for life?

The survivors of Hiroshima
and Nagasaki
are growing older.

Their message is clear:
Never again!

Wake up!
Now, before the feathered arrow
is placed into the bow.

Now, before the string
of the bow is pulled taut,
the arrow poised for flight.

Now, before the arrow is let loose,
before it flies across oceans
and continents.

Now, before we are engulfed in flames,
while there is still time, while we still can,
Wake up!

PEACE

So Few Even Know a Giant Has Died

for Mahmoud Darwish (1941-2008)

The olive trees still grow from the parched earth,
their trunks sturdy from standing against
the scorching sun and fierce wind.

The people still go about their business
of getting by on the arid land, of survival,
of song, of lament.

He was a man who spoke in love and simple words,
who grieved for the land that was taken
from him and his people.

When a giant dies, what are we to do
but count our blessings, remember one
who cared, and commit to do more.

Perhaps for this man there is only this:
look up from the dry earth and reach out
to a neighbor with kindness.

Kindness Conquers

for Francie Weissmuller

You often sat in dappled sunlight
drinking tea and contemplating beauty.

Your theory (you always had a theory)
was that harsh words and war
were reckless lunacy.

You carried your kindness gently,
like the petals of an ancient flower,
somehow still fragrant.

In time, your kindness became woven
into the fiber of your being, conquering
the complexity of our troubled world.

When you rose to dance among the stars
in the night sky, the petals of your ancient flower
floated slowly, softly back to Earth.

This Is What Peace Looks Like

Egypt, 2011

the people are in the streets and squares
making demands

the soldiers refuse to shoot their rifles
into the crowds

the people ride on army tanks
raising their arms with victory signs

the dictator is locked in his palace
knowing he has lost his grip

the people stand in the shadows
of Gandhi and King

the dictator cowers in the shadow
of his own history

The International Day of Peace

On this day, like any other,
soldiers are killing and dying,
arms merchants are selling their wares,
missiles are aimed at your heart,
and peace is a distant dream.

Not just for today, but for each day,
let's sheathe our swords, save the sky
for clouds, the oceans for mystery
and the Earth for joy.

Let's stop honoring the war makers
and start giving medals for peace.

On this day, like any other,
there are infinite possibilities to change
our ways.

Peace is an apple tree heavy with fruit,
a new way of loving the world.

Veterans Day Again

"The one thing I never want to see again
is a military parade."
                    ~Ulysses S. Grant

We've seen far too many military parades
with their missiles, marching bands
and mechanized young men.

We've witnessed enough high-stepping
soldiers in their polished black boots
marching to the sounds of brass.

Spare us the old men dressed in uniforms
with their sorrowful hats and sewn-on patches.
Spare us the slippery words of politicians.

Let's return to basics: On Armistice Day
the soldiers laid down their arms on the 11th hour
of the 11th day of the 11th month.

A generation was lost.
The survivors had had enough of war.
The 11th hour is here again, the sky clear blue.

PORTRAITS

The Maestro

The maestro, once a prodigy,
but now old, stands soldier straight
before the wall. On his lips and in his eyes,
the flicker of a smile.

The wall, bloodstained and riddled
with bullet holes, is filled with memories.
The maestro refuses a blindfold. For him,
everything is musical, even the song of death.

He is asked if he has any last words.
Of course, he says, far too many to share.
He tells a story about perfumed Wisteria,
vines that entangle a garden wall.

The soldiers with stoic faces
take their orders, aim and fire,
but their bullets make only dull thuds
against the wall, without harmony or power.

Even in death, the maestro's smile flickers.
His story hangs in the still air.

Last Meal

Before dawn, the general, surrounded by guards,
walked slowly across an open courtyard
toward the waiting gallows.

Suddenly he stopped and looked up at the sky.
The moon was full and he said to the guards,
"What a fair moon shines down on us."

He was a kindly man and the guards
were sorry for him. Swiftly the general
reached up, took hold of the moon and swallowed it.

"I will take this with me to the other side," he said.
After that, he walked on as though nothing unusual
had happened. He went to his death satisfied.

This took place in a time of peace
after a long and terrible war. The victors
kept busy judging the vanquished.

Einstein Sticks Out His Tongue

When asked for a pose, Einstein turned
toward the camera and stuck out his tongue.

He was captured on film, his white hair thinning
and awry, his dark eyes wild.

He was more than E equals MC squared, more
than his theories and gentle brilliance.

He was Albert. He was Einstein. He was
his own man, first and always.

He was lovely. He was real. And behind
his dark eyes, there was fear.

112 Mercer Street

God once lived at 112 Mercer Street.
Not a perfect God, but one with white hair
and an inquiring mind.

He was often disheveled and sometimes wore
only one sock. Still, he was able to create
quite an exceptional universe.

He loved his own secrets. He was forgetful
and occasionally had to rediscover his plan
for everything.

(Some wondered if he really had a plan.)

He said many wise things, except about women,
particularly his two wives. No one doubted
that he was clever.

On some days he liked being celebrated.
On other days, the evil in the world
was more than his shoulders could bear.

At night he would return to the house
on Mercer Street and sit in silence, pondering
the unfathomable mystery and majesty of it all.

Walter's Garden

The garden wasn't expansive
but it opened out to everywhere.
Its majestic oak touched the sky.

He loved to sit by the pond
in the dappled afternoon sunlight
contemplating unfathomable questions.

He carried these questions to a world
wholly unprepared for them,
a world too absorbed in violence.

The garden held many generations
of people, but he was its starting point.
Before him there was only history,

the ancient history of his boyhood.
In the garden his sons remembered him
recalling stories of determination.

It seemed possible he might return
with a smile, a shrug and a question.
It seemed possible he never left.

You Are Just So

for Charles Lloyd

You, my soft spoken friend
with your aspirations to Buddhahood,
with your "miles on the chassis,"

with your persistent insistence
that everything be just so,
including our intentions,

you, who travels so well
across continents and centuries
without wrinkles,

who jumps like a puppet
and lands like a cat,
soft, soft, on the sands of the shore,

who articulates your anger
in soulful sounds and rhythms
that awaken sleeping gods,

you are an artist of air
slender and shining,
elegant and intricate.

You are the professor who
professes with truth. You go
beyond making music.

You are music. You are just so.

A Veteran Recites Poetry on Veterans Day

The aging veteran, a stocky man with a broad face,
short white beard and a haunting question
in his eyes, reminds me of Socrates.

He had seen war close up in the jungles of Vietnam.
A 19-year-old rifleman, he was one of the fortunate ones
who came home alive.

A lot of his buddies, like Ephram, hadn't been
so lucky. So, in his poems, the old veteran
recalled Ephram and others who lost their lives for lies.

And for telling the truth, even these many years later,
the veteran, like Socrates, could be accused of corrupting
the youth, had there been some youth there to corrupt.

Jesse Jackson Sheds a Tear

A single tear shone on your cheek,
a tear that even you, especially you,
could not hold back.

You must have been thinking
of all it took to arrive at this moment
in America, of Rosa and Medgar,

of Martin and Malcolm, of the fire hoses,
the dogs, the lynchings, the four young girls
murdered in a Birmingham church,

of the long days struggling and marching
leading to the improbability of this moment
of possibility, and knowing through

your reverie that there is nothing,
no matter how implausible, that cannot be
forged of human dreams and will.

Madiba

How does one struggle for the freedom
of his people?
He showed us with his upraised fist.

How does one lead his fellow fighters
from within a small jail cell?
He showed us with his perseverance.

How does one extend the hand
of friendship to his jailers?
He showed us with his outstretched arm.

How does one emerge with dignity
after twenty-seven years in prison?
He showed us with his smile.

How does one forgive his oppressors
for the injustice of their crimes?
He showed us with his embrace of peace.

How does one walk courageously
toward peace with justice?
He showed us with his steady stride.

How does one come to love the world
and all its people?
He showed us with the fullness of his heart.

How does one earn the world's respect?
He showed us with his life.

IMPERFECTION

Imperfection

Looking at the helpless newborn
who was once me, my mother's friend
said to her, "Just think, someday
he will be a grandfather."

She forgot to add, "if he is lucky."
My mother just barely became
a grandmother before her luck
ran out.

Her friend, who had been with her
at my birth, lost her own daughter
in childbirth. After that nothing
much mattered to her.

Perfection, that grand, naïve idea,
is not a possibility, even at birth.
It recedes into the ether long before
we are aware its only form is mythic.

The best we can do is this: give love
and take time to polish our imperfection.

When I Learned about JFK

November 22, 1963

On a cold and crowded train platform in Kobe
as I rubbed my hands together and watched
my breath steam into the cold air, a young man
in a dark overcoat approached, and spoke in English,
"I'm sorry, your president has been shot and killed."
I was twenty-one years old and far from home.
The president had been shot and he, too, was far away.
Everything was about to change.

America would be drawn deeper into the war
in Vietnam, and I would be called into the army
and refuse to go to Vietnam. We would lose the war
and there would be other wars we would lose and America
would never be America again, at least not the America
I once believed was real.

Foreigner

I was always a foreigner
in your land,
but that is not strange.
I have been a foreigner
wherever I have been,
even where I was born.

You knew the customs
of the tribe
as though you had inherited them,
while I struggled to learn
the simplest greeting,
never at ease.

Your great gift
was your smile.
It grew from within,
attached to your sense
of belonging to wherever
you were.

You have never been away
from where you belong.
When it is time to dance,
you dance; when it is time
to sing, you sing.
You fit the terrain.

To be a foreigner
is to stand apart
by measured degrees
of detail and difference.
I have learned to smile
but I will never learn to sing.

Reflecting on You

Your soul, fully alive, has no sadness
from morning to night.

It is light and playful,
the soul of an innocent child.

Your soul is a hatchling, chirping
with joy, needing to be fed.

You are one of the fortunate ones,
never imagining what it means
to be lonely or frightened,

to be awakened in the night
and taken by the Gestapo.

On Hualalai

We drove up, up
through the pastureland,
past cows with calves
that watched us
with wide eyes
and scampered off,
past big bulls
that stood their ground,
past cock pheasant
and wild turkey
that wandered by.

We drove as far
as we could drive
and then walked on
through the thin air,
past the last Ohia trees
of the old forest.
We walked on
past the birds
with their sunny songs,
past the clouds.

As we walked on
into the depths
of the starlit sky,
we found ourselves
in the Big Dipper,
far bigger than
I imagined.

We curled up and slept
in a corner of its cup
and when the sky turned
we fell back to Earth, landing
on the soft green meadows
of Hualalai.

Dinner at Napoopoo

The old porch sways
under the weight of the sky,
Captain Cook's spirit
in the air.
Chicken and steak
sizzle on the grill,
the world far away.
Fire dances from torches.
White rice and salad.
Every simple thing is here.
Family. The restless sea.
Small boats of memory.
We drift across continents,
over wars of another time.
Fresh fish and soy sauce.
So much bounty.
Patter of rain on tin roof.
Sweet dark night.
Moon like a smile.
Coffee and starlight.

The Train from Nagasaki

The train from Nagasaki heads North through neatly shaped fields, passing farmhouses with their solid, gray tiled roofs, passing cities with their neatly ordered streets, passing factories and junkyards, passing magnificent trees that cover hillsides, traveling under the gray skies of Kyushu.

Long ago we took a bumpy train ride south to Nagasaki, traveling all night with our friend, Moriguchi, on our way to his wedding. We traveled into darkness as the train rolled methodically southward. We were young then, and there was nothing we couldn't do.

We've traveled over all these years, passing pleasures and sorrows, saying goodbyes to parents and friends, planting gardens and watching our children grow, somehow finding our way, keeping our roof tiled, our trees tended, and our hopes alive.

Fiftieth Reunion

The football star, with his full white beard,
has become a tired god. The cheerleader,
who married her high school sweetheart, has lived
the perfect suburban life.

The student body president
is a no show and cannot be found anywhere,
even on Google. The bookworm found his place,
lived a life of adventure.

Some have come from as far away as Sweden,
while others never left. There is a groping for words:
"So how has your life been for the past fifty years?"

We were once young together and cannot return.
If life were a game, we would be finishing
the third quarter and still behind.

We are the curious and fortunate ones, still
in the game.

Two Raccoons

Today we found two raccoons huddled
in the have-a-heart trap you had set
for whoever had been eating your begonias.

The raccoons were plump and furry.
They huddled so close together they seemed
like one animal with two heads and many paws.

As we lifted the trap into the back of our car
the raccoons became agitated and scrambled
about from one end of the trap to the other.

We drove them to the top of *Bella Vista* where
we parked the car overlooking a downward sloping
grassy meadow dotted with oak trees.

When we set the two raccoons free they scurried
across the meadow with no backward glances.
I doubt I've ever seen two happier creatures.

My Gifts

Though young, your smile was perfected.
Your laughter flowed like a clear stream.
Now, years have gone by, and you are still
as you were then, mistress to hummingbirds.

My form is always changing.
You have sensed in me the silence of the stars
and the tears in morning dew. I am unstable,
like mist or a lonely cloud.

I bring you honey and sweet ginger.
I roll a mighty stone up the hill again.
I bring you memories and an empty bowl.
I share with you my most prized collection
of imperfections.

We Walked Together

In fog, we walked along an empty beach,
above the water's edge, and looking back
along the shore, we saw our footprints
in the sand, like a patterned prayer.

We are here upon this rare Earth but once, we mused.
Conscious of our brief light within the fog
and the brevity of being, we breathed deep our bounty
and the ocean air, each taking our full share.

In eternity's long stretch of time,
behind us and ahead, we retraced our steps and
marveled that we should meet at all, let alone
here and now, in a place so fine and fair.

Small Bird

A small bird flew into our window
and fell stunned to the ground.

Without hesitation, you rushed outside,
cupped the frightened creature
in your hands and pressed it to your breast,
sharing your warmth with it.

The two of you exchanged heartbeats
while time paused in sacred silence
until the small bird was calmed and,
fluttering its wings, flew away.

Somber Mask

Each day I go to work behind a somber mask
seeking to achieve the Herculean task
of making of our species something greater
than perhaps we are, something that collectively
we've never been.

People ask, "What's all the fuss?"
They wonder why I raise my voice,
shouting yet again, "We have a choice."
"Oh, no," they say, "it's always been this way."

This does, however, miss the point.
The threat I see comes not from without
or from above, but from a logic starved of love.

Together we may choose to put away
atomic tools and threatening plans
of too bright men who are too certain
power rules. Or we may abstain.

Though late, we go on risking
our vaunted place on Earth.
Shall we succumb and maintain
this sullen face of churlish strength,
risking that we may become
the basic building blocks of unborn stars?
The common fate of humankind I say
resides within no other hands than ours.

Crying Wolf

There was a boy who cried wolf,
so to speak, running about saying,
"The sky is falling, the sky is falling."
But when people looked up, they saw
the sky, blue and tranquil, dotted
with clouds and it certainly was not falling.
The boy shouted for people to wake up,
but the people ignored the boy. They all
had busy lives, filled with their own fears.
They didn't worry the sky would fall, or
that it would explode, burying them
in edge-red ash.

In the end, the boy could only plead,
"Friends, help me catch the moon."

Still Hope

As we stood in the kitchen sipping
our morning veggie drinks and talking
about how routines, like tea ceremony or karate,
opened doors of creativity, I noticed through the window
a tightly-packed red camellia bud and pointed it out to you.
You smiled and said, "There's still hope."

Each New Year

another revolution
around the sun

a moment of pause
to take account

a fresh beginning
to make our world right

another chance to be
a good citizen of Earth

new hope that love
may conquer fear

Tenacity

It has been raining steadily through the night and
continues through the morning. The small creek
I can see through my window, the one
that is dry most of the year, the creek
in which our children played when they were young,
launching twigs and small boats on its rough waters,
the creek that amazed us when we were young, as so
many things did, is running hard. Its sound
is strong and vital. Beyond the creek, the green
is very green and the red azalea blossoms smile
and hang on.

Zen Is...

I.

the freedom of imperfection
an incomplete circle
reflections on silence
infinity in a speck of dust
poems without syllables
bombs without triggers
a flight through the universe
dew on a blade of grass
an open door
breath on a mirror
the power of moonlight
time enough

II.

to prefer a circle
less than perfect
spontaneously drawn
in black ink
by a man
with a wispy
gray beard
a circle
with ragged edges
and a splattering
of black ink
on a white canvas
to a well tailored
corporate swoosh
to almost anything

So Much More

The yellow tulip turns its head.

There's so much more that could be said.

ACKNOWLEDGMENTS

My deep appreciation to:

Blase Bonpane, co-founder and director of the Office of the Americas. He is a former priest and a moral beacon in our world of war, injustice and suffering.

Paul K. Chappell, my colleague at the Nuclear Age Peace Foundation, the Director of our Peace Leadership Program. He applies the leadership skills he learned at West Point to the quest for peace. His latest book is *The Art of Waging Peace*.

Richard Falk, Professor Emeritus of International Law and Practice at Princeton University. He is a wise man and a friend who never shies away from speaking truth to power.

Lawrence Ferlinghetti, a leading American poet and a co-founder of City Lights Booksellers & Publishers. He says, "If you would be a poet, create works capable of answering the challenge of apocalyptic times...."

Perie Longo, a former Poet Laureate of Santa Barbara and a dear friend in poetry. Her latest book of poems, rich in wisdom and finely crafted, is entitled *Baggage Claim*.

Mairead Maguire, a Nobel Peace Laureate from Northern Ireland. Her experience in Northern Ireland and receiving the Nobel Peace Prize have motivated her to a lifetime of activities for peace throughout the world.

Glenn Paige, the founder of the Center for Global Non-Killing. He is an academic who has been transformed by a vision of a non-killing world into a secular saint.

Doug Rawlings, a poet and Vietnam War veteran who knows the price of war. He is a co-founder of Veterans for Peace. His new and superb collection of poems is entitled *Orion Rising*.

Stuart Rees, a poet and founder of Sydney Peace Foundation. His latest collection of peace poetry is entitled *A Will to Live*.

Gerry Spence, a leading trial lawyer, writer and dear friend, who has always encouraged me to be the best person and poet I can be.

Desmond Tutu, a Nobel Peace Laureate and Archbishop Emeritus of Cape Town, South Africa. He is one of the leading moral voices in the world today.

Carol Warner, my assistant at the Nuclear Age Peace Foundation, who has been helpful in innumerable ways.

My wife, Carolee, who has supported my work for peace and my poetry since we were young.

The Board, Advisors, staff and members of the Nuclear Age Peace Foundation, a vibrant community seeking to build a more secure and decent world, who contribute daily to awakening humanity to standing firmly for peace, justice and a world free of nuclear weapons.

AUTHOR

David Krieger is a peace leader and poet. He is a founder of the Nuclear Age Peace Foundation, and has served as President of the Foundation since 1982. He has lectured throughout the United States, Europe and Asia on issues of peace, security, international law, and the abolition of nuclear weapons. He serves as an advisor to many peace organizations around the world and has received many awards for his work for a more peaceful and nuclear weapons-free world.

Dr. Krieger is the author or editor of numerous studies of peace in the Nuclear Age. Among his books are several poetry volumes, including: *Summer Grasses: An Anthology of War Poetry* (editor); *Never Enough Flowers: The Poetry of Peace II* (editor); *God's Tears: Reflections on the Atomic Bombs Dropped on Hiroshima and Nagasaki*; *The Doves Flew High*; *Today Is Not a Good Day for War*; and *The Poetry of Peace* (editor).

He is a graduate of Occidental College, and holds MA and Ph.D. degrees in political science from the University of Hawaii as well as a J.D. from the Santa Barbara College of Law.

NUCLEAR AGE PEACE FOUNDATION

The Nuclear Age Peace Foundation is a non-profit, non-partisan international organization. Since 1982, it has initiated and supported worldwide efforts to enhance both global and human security and is a voice for millions of people concerned about the fate of the planet. The Foundation has consultative status to the United Nations Economic and Social Council and is recognized by the UN as a Peace Messenger Organization.

Vision

Our vision is a just and peaceful world, free of nuclear weapons.

Mission

To educate and advocate for peace and a world free of nuclear weapons, and to empower peace leaders.

Contact

Nuclear Age Peace Foundation
PMB 121, 1187 Coast Village Road, Suite 1
Santa Barbara, CA 93108-2794
Telephone: (805) 965-3443
Fax: (805) 568-0466
E-mail: dkrieger@napf.org

Web Presence

We invite you to learn more about the Foundation's programs by visiting our websites.
www.wagingpeace.org | www.nuclearfiles.org | www.nuclearzero.org

Made in the USA
Middletown, DE
02 April 2015